THE
CHUMASH
INDIANS

THE JUNIOR LIBRARY OF
AMERICAN INDIANS

THE CHUMASH INDIANS

Martin Schwabacher

CHELSEA JUNIORS

a division of CHELSEA HOUSE PUBLISHERS

FRONTISPIECE: Chumash elder Rafael Solares displays the traditional costume of the *antap*, a Chumash religious society.

CHAPTER TITLE ORNAMENT: A drawing similar to a Chumash painting found in a remote location at the base of a 75-foot rock with carved footholds leading to the top.

English-language words that are italicized in the text can be found in the glossary at the back of the book.

Chelsea House Publishers
EDITORIAL DIRECTOR Richard Rennert
EXECUTIVE MANAGING EDITOR Karyn Gullen Browne
COPY CHIEF Robin James
PICTURE EDITOR Adrian G. Allen
ART DIRECTOR Robert Mitchell
MANUFACTURING DIRECTOR Gerald Levine
ASSISTANT ART DIRECTOR Joan Ferrigno

The Junior Library of American Indians
SENIOR EDITOR Martin Schwabacher

Staff for THE CHUMASH INDIANS
ASSOCIATE EDITOR David Shirley
COPY EDITOR Catherine Iannone
EDITORIAL ASSISTANTS Annie McDonnell, Sydra Mallery
DESIGNER John Infantino
PICTURE RESEARCHER Villette Harris
COVER ILLUSTRATOR Hal Just

5 7 9 8 6

Library of Congress Cataloging-in-Publication Data

Schwabacher, Martin.
The Chumash Indians/Martin Schwabacher.
  p. cm. — (The Junior library of American Indians)
Includes index.
        0-7910-2488-1
        0-7910-2490-3 (pbk.)
1. Chumash Indians—Juvenile literature. I. Title. II. Series.
E99.C815S38 1995   94-17181
979.4'01—dc20   CIP
                                                              AC

CONTENTS

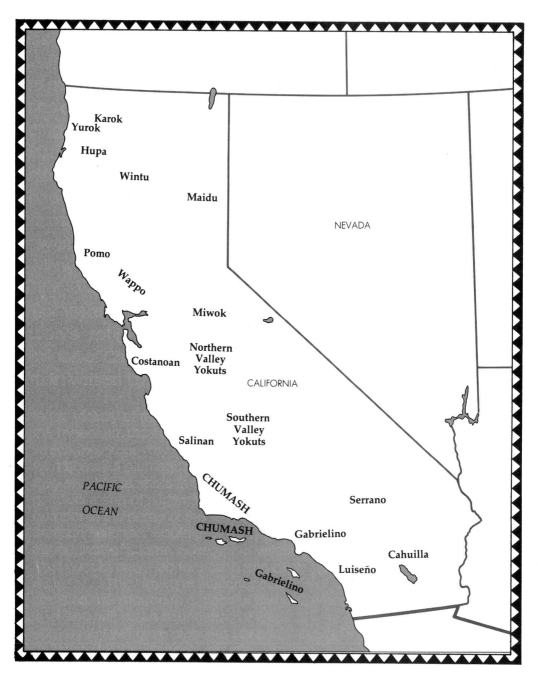

Karok
Yurok
Hupa
Wintu
Maidu
NEVADA
Pomo
Wappo
Miwok
Northern
Valley
Yokuts
Costanoan
CALIFORNIA
Southern
Valley
Yokuts
Salinan
PACIFIC
OCEAN
CHUMASH
Serrano
CHUMASH
Gabrielino
Cahuilla
Gabrielino
Luiseño

The Chumash lived on a 150-mile stretch of land along the coast of the Pacific Ocean around Santa Barbara. The area was both beautiful and rich in natural resources, and the Chumash were able to develop a complex and thriving society.

CHAPTER 1

The First Californians

Thousands of people drive down the crowded highways of Southern California every day. Yet very few of these busy commuters realize that many of the roads they are driving on were built along paths made by the Chumash Indians thousands of years ago.

Today there is very little left of the people who lived and thrived in California before the arrival of smog and automobiles. But these Native Americans lived in California for a far, far longer time than modern-day Americans have. Los Angeles, today a teeming city of millions, has existed for barely 200 years. Yet

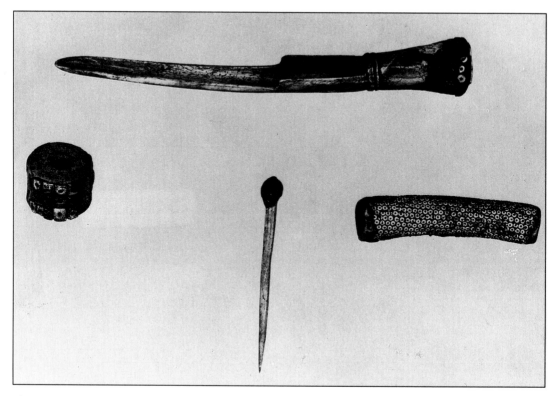

the Chumash and their ancestors lived for a hundred *centuries* on the land where modern roads and cities now lie.

Less than 100 miles up the coast from Los Angeles is the city of Santa Barbara. An hour's drive to the east looms the Sierra Nevada range. To the west, across the Santa Barbara Channel, there are four islands: San Miguel, Santa Rosa, Santa Cruz, and tiny Anacapa Island. For thousands of years, these islands and the 150-mile stretch of coastline around Santa Barbara were the home of the Chumash Indians.

The Chumash used bone and bits of shell to fashion jewelry and utensils. Above are pictured beads (left and right), an awl (bottom), and a hair ornament (top) decorated with inlaid shell beads.

No one knows what the Chumash called themselves before the first Spanish settlers arrived in what is now California. The white settlers gave the Indians the name by which they are known to this day. The Indians' name for Santa Rosa Island was *Tcúmac*; they called Santa Cruz Island *Mitcúmac*. The Spaniards probably heard one of these words and mistakenly thought it referred to all the Indians in the surrounding area.

The words *Tcúmac* and *Mitcúmac* probably came from the Indian word *alchum*, meaning money. Chumash money consisted of strings of tiny shell beads that were made by hand. The island Indians were the ones who made this money, because they were the only ones who could gather the correct shells.

Only one kind of shell was used to make alchum: the purple olivella. The shells were broken into several pieces, which were chipped into circles. These were then stirred in hot coals until they turned white. Next, holes were drilled in the round chips using a sharp piece of bone or stone attached to a thin stick. The beads were then polished and strung. Each string was long enough to wrap once around a person's hand. When someone wanted to buy something, the price was given in strings of beads.

Many Indian societies never used money; people made what they needed themselves or traded with one another. The Chumash, however, started using money more than 1,000 years ago. They needed a money system because their society was very complex. Because they lived in different surroundings with different natural resources, Chumash people tended to specialize in making one thing. There were people who specialized in making beads, headdresses, tobacco, nets, baskets, leather, tools, and canoes. They had to buy and sell from each other to get the other goods they needed. Craftspeople formed groups that set the prices for their products.

The trading formed bonds between distant villages. Because different regions were better suited to producing different things, trading benefited everybody. People in island villages caught fish and gathered shells. Those who lived in the forest hunted for meat and collected acorns, which were the Chumash's most important food. At regularly held fairs, people from all parts of the Chumash nation would gather to trade.

The trading extended far beyond the boundaries of the Chumash territory. Steatite, a soft stone that the Chumash used to carve bowls and sculptures, was obtained from

The shell of the abalone, or sea mollusk, can be found in abundance along the Pacific coast. Abalone shells are both beautiful and strong, and they were used by the Chumash to make everything from fish hooks to earrings.

the Gabrielino Indians of Santa Catalina Island, just south of Los Angeles. Traders from more distant tribes—some as far as 400 miles away—brought obsidian, a glassy black rock that was chipped into sharp knives and arrowheads.

A member of the Yokuts Indians, the tribe just to the southeast of the Chumash, described a meeting with "the bead and sea-shell traders from the coast." These traders were almost certainly Chumash.

> The people who wanted to trade carried their things in baskets on their backs. They had to have their *Teah* (chief) with them. When they came up to trade they marched up in a straight line from each side. The *Teah* was in front.
>
> When the two parties got close to each other they all took hold of the basket straps at the sides of their heads and swung from side to side, singing:
>
> *Ho-hoo-hoo Yoo-nah* (sung five times)
>
> *Hah-Ha*
>
> *He-ke-mah* was the name of that song. That was the name of the trade too.
>
> When the song was done each took his basket down and spread his things on the ground in front of him. The rows of things were about ten feet apart. Then the trade started. The *Teahs* did all the talking for the people. They talked to each other and agreed how much each could have. It was all done by rules.

The Chumash leaders, who could be either men or women, were called *wots*. Each village controlled certain areas that were used for hunting or gathering food. The wots decided whether to allow other villages to use their territory. These villages would later have to perform some service in return, such as hosting a festival. During severe food shortages, a council of village wots would decide how to divide the available food so that all the Chumash people would have enough to eat.

The first Europeans who came to California were impressed by the Chumash's business skills. Antonio Fages, a Spanish missionary who visited the Chumash in 1769, observed, "They are inclined to work, and much more to self-interest. . . . In matters concerning their possessions, they will not yield or concede the smallest point."

Unfortunately for the Chumash, Fages and other missionaries came to stay. They built settlements called *missions* and forced the Indians to work for them. They also made the Chumash give up their own religion and become Catholics. In a very short time, the society the Chumash had built over thousands of years was destroyed.

But to those who look for them, there are still signs of the old ways. High in the mountains, or hidden in rocky caves along the coast, strange and exotic pictures can be found. What they mean remains a mystery; those who once knew are long dead. But a tiny group of Chumash Indians still survives. Today, some of the modern Chumash work as *archaeologists*, unearthing and preserving the history of their ancestors. ▲

Chumash elder Rafael Solares (photographed by Leon de Cessac during the late 19th century) uses traditional tools to make arrowheads and spearpoints out of stone.

CHAPTER 2

A Complex Society

Southern California, especially along the coast of the Pacific Ocean, is one of the most beautiful and comfortable places to live in the whole world. Temperatures are mild year-round, and there is always plenty of sun. Each year, the region attracts visitors and immigrants from all over the world. As long as people have known about California, it seems, people have wanted to live there.

The very first settlers came between 27,000 and 12,000 years ago. Before that, not a single human being lived anywhere in North America. Then, during a period called the Ice Age, the world grew cold. Giant glaciers stretched for hundreds of miles. So much of the water in the ocean was frozen into glaciers that the sea lowered, revealing a strip of land connecting Asia and Alaska. This land bridge allowed people to walk for the first time from Asia to North America.

Once human beings had reached North America, they quickly multiplied and spread across the continent. Eventually, the lucky travelers who slowly made their way toward the Pacific coast found the sunny shores of California. Many of them settled there to live.

Some of the tools made by the Chumash's ancestors have been discovered by archaeologists, scientists who dig up and study signs of people who lived long ago. Very near Santa Barbara, archaeologists found remains of villages 10,000 years old. Several of the oldest discoveries were flat stones used to mill, or grind, seeds into flour. Because the archaeologists found so many of these milling stones in the area, they called the early settlers Millingstone people.

Around 5,000 years ago, the climate in Southern California changed. Giant forests grew in abundance, and instead of seeds, people began to gather and eat more and more acorns. With this more stable source of food, villages grew larger. Village chiefs grew wealthier, and their societies grew more complex. By about 3,000 years ago, the Chumash civilization had emerged.

The first European explorer to visit the Chumash arrived on October 10, 1542, when a Spanish expedition led by Juan Rodriguez Cabrillo sailed into the Santa Barbara Channel. Cabrillo named the first village he visited Las Canoas because of the vast number of canoes owned by the Indians there. A member of the expedition, Juan Paez, kept a diary of the voyage. His diary recorded the first encounter between Chumash and non-Indians. "Here there came to the ships very many canoes," he wrote, "each of which held twelve or thirteen Indians." The Spanish ships moved on and anchored "in front of a magnificent valley densely populated, with level land, and many *groves*." Paez continued,

> Here came canoes with fish to *barter*; the Indians were very friendly . . . all the way there were many canoes . . . and many Indians kept boarding the ships. They pointed out the pueblos (villages) and told us their names.

Later expeditions caught further glimpses of a thriving Indian community. The Spanish encountered dozens of villages eager to trade with them. Although no one knows the exact number, one source recorded 191 villages in the Santa Barbara area alone and 23 more villages on the islands. According to another estimate, a total of 20;000 to 30,000 Chumash people lived in 75 to 100 villages.

By all accounts, the Chumash were friendly and generous to the visitors. Father Juan Crespi wrote in 1769, "As soon as we arrived all the people came to visit us and brought a great supply of roasted fish until the canoes arrived with fresh ones." Crespi wrote that they were so generous that "it was necessary to tell them not to bring any more for it would eventually have to spoil."

Because of the mild weather, Chumash men wore almost no clothing, and the women usually wore only a skirt. Instead they decorated their bodies with paint and jewlery. Paez described the men's hair as "very long and tied up with long strings interwoven with the hair, there being attached to the strings many gewgaws of flint, bone and wood."

Another writer described the Indians as "well formed and of good body." "Some of them," the same writer observed, "have the cartilage of the nose pierced, and all have the ears perforated with two large holes in which they wear little canes like two horns as thick as the little finger . . . in which they are accustomed to carry powder made of their wild tobacco."

This sketch of a Chumash village during the early mission period was made by contemporary artist Russel Ruiz. In the foreground are several tomols, or plank canoes.

Fages reported that in each village he visited there were two or three men who lived and dressed as women, and that they were treated with great respect.

In 1792, the Spanish government sent a naturalist named José Longinos Martínez to make a survey of the land where the Chumash lived. Martínez spent a month among the Chumash, taking detailed notes. His observations provide a firsthand account of the Chumash before their society was

completely altered by the European presence. Describing the appearance of the Chumash women, Martínez wrote:

> The dress and adornment of the women was
> graceful. From the waist down they usually wear
> two very soft pieces of buckskin, the edges of
> which are cut into fringes and ornamented with
> strings of beads, snail shells and others of various
> colors which give a very pretty effect. One of
> these skins is worn in front and the other behind.
> . . . They adorn their heads tastefully with
> necklaces and earrings. Their hair is worn in
> bangs cut short and combed forward . . . they
> trim it daily by singeing it hair by hair with a
> piece of pine bark so that no hair protrudes. . . .
> Their headdress or *coiffure* gives the women
> a neat and graceful appearance.

Martínez also noted that the Indians painted
their bodies with red *ocher*. Each village used
a different pattern to distinguish itself from
the others.

The Chumash lived in domed houses of
varying size. A single-family house could be
as little as 12 or 15 feet wide and 5 feet high,
but some houses were much bigger. Huge
50-foot buildings could be used to house 50
or more people.

Houses were built by driving willow poles
into the ground, then bending the tops together to form a dome. The larger buildings
had extra poles supporting the middle. More
poles were woven sideways through the

vertical poles and tied with strips of bark. Mats of woven reeds were then attached to the pole structure like shingles, making walls and a waterproof roof. A hole in the center of the roof allowed smoke to escape.

Martínez's writings provide a detailed description of the Chumash's living quarters:

> These Indians live in communities and have a fixed domicile. They arrange their houses in groups. The houses are well constructed, round like an oven, spacious and fairly comfortable; light enters through a hole in the roof. Their beds are made on frames and they cover themselves with skins and shawls. The beds have divisions between them like the cabins of a ship, so that if many people sleep in one house, they do not see one another. In the middle of the floor they make a fire for cooking seeds, fish and other foods, for they eat everything boiled or roasted. Next to their houses they build smaller ones in which to store seeds, dried fish, sardines and other things against the winter when the cold, rain and roughness of the sea prevent foraging.

Some of these storehouses were on stilts, to keep the preserved food off the ground and away from hungry animals. The largest of these structures were used to store acorns, the Chumash's most important food. These storehouses could hold as much as 1,000 pounds of nuts.

Acorns, the nutritious nuts of the oak tree, were quite abundant; the Chumash simply had to collect them in the forest each fall. Acorns are extremely bitter, however, because they contain a great deal of tannic acid. To remove the tannic acid, Chumash women removed the shells from the acorns and pounded the nuts into powder. They then put the acorn flour in woven baskets and poured water over it. The water seeped out of the baskets, taking the tannic acid with it. This was repeated several times until the acorns tasted good enough to eat. The flour was then eaten as mush or baked into little cakes that were flavored with spices, meat, or berries.

The Chumash ate many different plant foods, including the flowers, leaves, seeds, roots, and bulbs of various plants. Because of the moderate climate, plants could be collected year-round. During the spring, the Chumash collected seeds and flowers. During the summer dry season, they gathered fruits, berries, and deep roots. In fall, the larger bushes and trees bore nuts and berries, supplying acorns, pine nuts, wild strawberries, and cattail seeds. When the winter rains arrived, they collected bulbs, roots, and fresh leaves, such as clover, mustard greens, and other herbs. Thus they always had fresh seeds, fruits, or vegetables in addition to the food they kept in their storehouses.

The ocean provided an endless supply of fish for the people who lived near the coast. They fished from canoes, using harpoons, nets, and fishhooks. Chumash people who lived farther inland caught fish from the rivers. One *ingenious* method for catching fish in still water involved the soaproot plant. When pounded fresh and sprinkled on the water, the plant paralyzed the gills of fish. The fish would float to the surface, where the Chumash collected them.

Shellfish could be gathered year-round on the islands and along the coast. They were evidently an important source of food—heaps of empty shells 20 feet tall have been *excavated* near ancient Chumash villages.

The Chumash also hunted several kinds of animals. Rabbits and squirrels were killed with bows and arrows, thrown clubs, or slingshots, or they were caught with nets. Sometimes the Chumash drove rabbits into the open by lighting the brush on fire. Smaller animals such as mice and gophers could be caught by digging up their burrows. Turtles, frogs, and lizards were also eaten.

Many animals were caught by trickery. Birds such as ducks were attracted by wooden decoys carved to look like birds. When the ducks landed near the decoys, the Chumash tossed a net over them. Sometimes hunters placed food under a rock propped up by a stick, then pulled the stick out with a string when an animal such as a rabbit crawled under the rock. The Chumash were also skilled stalkers of their prey. When hunting deer, the Chumash dressed in deerskin and antlers, then quietly approached until they were close enough to kill the animals with an arrow or stone-tipped spear. Some witnesses claimed that Chumash hunters could run down a deer on foot.

The dangerous grizzly bear was very difficult to kill, and Chumash hunters wisely avoided the huge and ferocious adult bears. Sometimes, however, the Chumash would catch young cubs and fatten them up to eat later.

Insects and insect larvae also contributed to the Chumash diet. The Chumash obtained sugar in the form of honeydew, an excretion of aphids and other insects. When aphids swarmed on carrizo grass in the summer, the tiny green insects left the grass coated with honeydew, which dried into crystals. The Chumash cut the grass and shook off the honeydew, which they then pressed into balls like lumps of maple sugar.

The Chumash also liked to eat insects, the most popular being the grasshopper. Grasshoppers would sometimes appear in

The Chumash were particularly skilled weavers—some of their baskets were woven so tightly that they held water. These traditional baskets were made by interweaving dyed black twine among the natural fibers.

huge swarms, and everyone would turn out to catch them. One effective method was to build a fire in a pit and wait until it burned down into coals. Then as many people as possible would form a large circle around the hot coals. They would gradually tighten the circle, beating the ground with branches to drive the grasshoppers ahead of them until the insects jumped into the fire pit, where they were instantly roasted. The dried insects were then strung on sticks and eaten as a crunchy snack, or they were ground up and mixed with hot acorn mush. Dried grasshoppers provided an important source of nutrition in the winter months.

The Chumash did not make clay pottery, but they made excellent stone containers and woven baskets. Chumash weavers were considered some of the finest basketmakers in America. Some baskets were woven so tightly that they were waterproof. Any basket could be made waterproof, however, by coating the inside with a naturally occurring tar called asphalt. Bits of asphalt were placed in the basket, then hot rocks were rolled around inside, melting and spreading the asphalt to provide a smooth, even seal.

In certain places asphalt oozed out of the ground like water from a spring, and the Chumash were fortunate to have several of these wells in their territory. Asphalt was a useful item for exchange with other tribes. The Chumash also used it for many things, including gluing beads to decorative objects and waterproofing canoes. It was even used as chewing gum.

The Chumash made several different types of canoes. Some, used for short trips, were made of bundles of reeds. Others were made by hollowing out a single log by burning part of it with hot rocks and chopping out the charcoal. But the most impressive canoe by far was the *tomol*, or plank canoe, made from many separate boards. Flat rectangles of wood were made by splitting pieces of driftwood and scraping them until they were three-quarters of an inch thick. These were then sanded with pieces of sharkskin. Next, small holes were drilled in the boards, which were sewn together with string made from plant fiber. Finally, all the holes and cracks were sealed with tar. Tomols carried 6 to 12 people and were typically 30 feet long. These large canoes could travel long distances on the open seas, easily making the 30-mile trip between the mainland and the channel islands.

Although the food, shelter, and clothing of the Chumash were very different from those used today in California, their material possessions give only a hint of how different their way of life was from that of present-day California. Socially, politically, and spiritually, the Chumash lived in a completely different world. ▲

The Chumash performed this 2,000-year-old dance to honor swordfish, which they believed helped them by driving whales to their shores.

CHAPTER 3

The Spirit World

From birth to death to the afterlife, the Chumash looked at everything from a religious perspective. They believed that every object had spiritual power, from the food they gathered to the animals they hunted to the rocks they used for tools. Supernatural beings were believed to play an active role in the Chumash's world. This was also true of the strange creatures the Chumash encountered in their dreams. The Chumash's religion helped them make peace with these spirits in all their daily tasks and rituals.

According to a Chumash myth, the world was made up of three layers. The top layer rested on the wings of a giant eagle. In this

A chumash belief is that babies had to be born where their mothers went to labor

shaman was useful

...Chumash were ...s at working ...tite, a soft, ...rown stone ...they made ...ly objects including ...als and animal ...te ...here ...e long before ...first white settlers arrived in Chumash territory.

layer lived powerful supernatural beings, including the Moon, the Morning Star, and the Sun. People lived in the middle layer. Underneath the human world lived dangerous creatures who crept aboveground at night.

Certain important supernatural beings were known as First People. The Chumash believed that some of them once lived among humans. Later, the First People became the animals, plants, and natural forces such as thunder. Because these spirits lived on in the form of everyday objects, the Chumash believed it was always important to thank the spirits for all the natural things they used. Numerous rituals kept the Chumash in harmony with these spirits and powerful natural forces.

One Chumash belief was that babies had to be born in the exact spot where their mothers went into labor. When a woman felt her first birth pains, she dug a hole in the ground precisely where she was standing. She warmed the hole with hot rocks and lined it with straw. When the baby was born, she broke its nose and flattened it to make it more beautiful. Then a *shaman*, a person with great spiritual power, named the child. The appropriate name could bring the child good luck.

Children had their own rituals to follow. When they reached puberty, for example, girls were not allowed to look into a fire. The most important puberty ritual for boys and girls involved taking *toloache*, a drug made from the jimsonweed plant that caused them to have visions. With the help of a shaman, the young people would drink toloache and fall into a dream state. Then they would meet a spirit, who would become their guide and helper for the rest of their life. By interpreting the dream, the shaman could predict their future.

Powerful shamans often had more than one spirit helper. A guide could be the soul of a dead person—usually another shaman—

or an animal spirit. Shamans also used magic charms, such as rattles, whistles, feathers, and smooth cigar-shaped stones. One of the main skills of the shaman was to cure disease. This could be done by sucking the illness out of a sick person with a special tube.

The Chumash also believed that certain kinds of shamans had special powers. Rain doctors could control the weather; rattlesnake doctors protected against snakebite; and bear doctors could turn into grizzly bears.

Anthropologist John P. Harrington wrote down many Chumash stories, including several about bear shamans. Juan de Jesus Justo, a Chumash Indian, told Harrington, "Wizards or sorcerers would have two bear paws hanging around their necks. They would throw these into a thicket and the paws would have to fight with a wild bear."

Fernando Librado, another Chumash Indian, told how bear shamans would kill a bear and take off its skin in a single piece. The shamans would then stuff the skin with grass to preserve its shape. After doing this, they would climb inside the skin. With the help of supernatural forces, the bear shamans could travel great distances very quickly. Librado

continued on page 41

CENTURIES OF CHUMASH ART

The fertile shores of southern California made food collection relatively easy, freeing Chumash artisans to specialize in various crafts. Their everyday tools and ceremonial objects were both beautiful and skillfully made. Chumash artisans were known as some of the finest basket makers in the world. They also carved beautiful bowls and sculptures out of stone. The Chumash's centuries-old tradition of artistic excellence continues to the present day.

A painting by modern-day artist Russel A. Ruiz of a coastal Chumash village as it would have looked in the late 16th century. A Spanish sailing vessel is anchored offshore in the background.

In the foreground of this Ruiz painting, set in 1795, four Chumash men paddle a tomol, or plank canoe, a type of boat unique to the Chumash. On the mainland are a Chumash village and, behind it, the buildings of Mission Santa Bárbara. In the background, a brush fire rages across the hills.

The chapel of Cieneguitas and the Chumash village of Kaswa, painted in the 1930s by Henry S. Ford. The settlement was established as a satellite of Mission Santa Bárbara so that the mission system could control a wider area of Chumash territory.

A series of Chumash rock paintings found in the hills of the tribe's southern California homeland. These works of art were expressions of Chumash religious beliefs and may have been made by shamans or other powerful people as acts of communion with the spirit world.

Reconstructed fragments of several bowls made from serpentine. The large bowl in the rear was apparently broken by its Chumash owner, who repaired it by drilling holes along the broken edges and then sewing them together with leather strips.

A storage bowl and a traditional frying pan, both made from steatite.

The bottom of a broken steatite bowl in which the Chumash mixed asphaltum, a waterproof substance. Inside the bowl are an asphaltum cake and the stone that was used to apply it to other objects.

Two prehistoric canoe effigies made from steatite. These miniature boats were used as charms by Chumash fishermen to ensure good luck during fishing expeditions. According to Chumash elder Fernando Librado, "when a canoe charm dreamer dies, [his] effigy canoes . . . are buried with him. The little boats which are found in such a grave are no longer of value, for their owner is dead, and [only] he knew how to manipulate the charms."

continued from page 32

explained how bear shamans controlled their magic powers:

> There were three cords inside the skin with loops for each of three fingers. The index finger makes the bear walk, the middle finger makes it run, and the ring finger makes it turn. The index and middle fingers together cause the bear to go very swiftly, and if you don't know the combination you are likely to go too fast and bump up against the side of a tree or a mountain or something.

One custom that all the Chumash men took part in was the daily use of *temescales,* or sweat lodges. These huts were partly underground, and they were covered with mud to hold in the heat from a large fire. The only opening was a hole in the roof. Chumash men would climb down a pole and sit around the fire, sweating. After soaping up their bodies with soaproot, they would sing songs and rub the sweat off their bodies with bone scrapers. Afterward they would run outside and jump into the ocean or a cold river. They performed this ritual to purify the mind and body. Chumash men would also use sweat lodges before a hunt. After they were totally clean, they rubbed their skin with herbs and oils to hide any remaining scent.

Twice a year, all the Chumash villages would meet for a giant gathering, which the Spanish called a fiesta. The assembled

Indians would buy and sell goods, play games, dance, sing, and gamble. The host village's wot would provide food that he or she had collected from the rest of the village. The organizer of the gathering was the *paxa*, the second highest ranking leader of the village. The paxa made announcements, gave speeches, and collected money and gifts for the wot. The paxa was also in charge of the religious ceremonies and dances performed at the fiesta.

All the dancers were members of a religious society called the *antap*. Members of the antap joined the society as children. Because it cost a great deal of money to join the antap, all of the members came from wealthy families. When they were accepted, children learned sacred songs, dances, and a secret language.

The antap rituals thanked important First People, such as Hutash, the Earth, and Kakunupmawa, the Sun. If they were not treated with respect, the First People might allow the Chumash to starve. All the Chumash, not just the antap, had to behave correctly every day in order to keep the world in balance.

Fiestas also provided an opportunity to arrange marriages. If a man wanted to marry a woman, he had to pay a great deal of money to the woman's family. People who wished

Ancient Chumash rock paintings still decorate many of the caves and hillsides of Southern California. These mysterious paintings expressed the religious beliefs of the Chumash people.

to remarry after the death of a husband or wife were only allowed to marry other widows and widowers.

Some of the most intriguing artifacts left by the Chumash are their strange and colorful rock paintings. The Chumash made paints of many different colors by grinding up minerals and mixing them with egg whites, animal fat, or milkweed sap. Chumash artists, probably shamans, painted on the walls of caves in the mountains and other remote locations. Mixed with abstract symbols are drawings of many strange creatures: head-

continued on page 46

Many of the stories told by the Chumash were preserved by ethnologist John P. Harrington (1884–1961). Harrington spent several years between 1912 and 1928 living among the Chumash and writing down the stories told to him by the oldest members of the community, who still knew the Chumash language and remembered Chumash myths and folktales. The following descriptions of the nunašɨš, the mysterious creatures who come aboveground during the night, were told to Harrington and later published in December's Child: A Book of Chumash Oral Narratives *(1975), edited by Thomas C. Blackburn.*

The Nunašɨš

The nunašɨš are creatures of the other world that come out soon after nightfall and travel all around. The old people used to say that you should bathe early before they return from going around the world, for later the water is steaming because they bathe in it. The haphap is nunašɨš—he has the form of a man, but he is very dangerous and very devilish. When he inhales he draws trees and rocks and everything toward himself and swallows them. Ququ, lewelew, yowoyow, and the manunašɨš pakaʔs asʔil—the lame devil whose leg is broken and who goes hopping around the world—all have human form also. Ququ and lewelew have bodies covered with pus, and their facial skin is loose. The yowoyow is similar. He lives at a certain place down near Ventura, and the people there see his smoke rising some times. And the people around here believe in La Llorona, the maxulaw or mamismis, that cries up in the trees like a newborn baby. Once a man saw one: it looks like a cat, but with skin like leather or rawhide. When you hear it someone is going to die. It is strange that you don't see La Llorona anymore. And the xolxol are big animals covered with feathers, and the feathers make a noise when they move. The late Rafael wrestled with the lewelew once. He was with his wife at the time. He jumped out of bed suddenly and his wife lit a candle. He was swaying and staggering around the room. He finally fell down exhausted, and his wife asked, "What's wrong with you, are you crazy?" At first he couldn't answer, but he finally got his breath back and said, "What else can you expect wrestling with the lewelew?" What a thing to happen!

continued from page 43

less people, leaping figures, creatures that resemble insects, and flying animals. Many are part human and part animal, or combinations of different animals, or totally unknown beings. Other pictures look like stars, comets, or wheels. Although some of the ancient paintings have been vandalized by visitors, dozens of remote cliffs and caverns in Chumash territory still bear these mysterious drawings.

Many details of the Chumash's religious beliefs were kept secret from the Spanish, who were intent on wiping out the Chumash's religion. However, a *tantalizing* glimpse of Chumash beliefs can be seen in a report written by a missionary in 1815:

> In the vicinity of their rancherias (villages) and on the mountain, they used to have some place which they kept very clean, swept and adorned with beautiful plumage put on poles. . . . Here they would assemble in time of need and conduct a sort of pilgrimage. One of their number in the name of the rest who observed profound silence, would pray for rain offering an abundance of acorns, seeds, and wild fruits. . . . They would pray also for health and other good things. . . . They imagine that after death, the souls are transferred to a place of delights where . . . there will be an abundance of fish and where they will have plenty to eat and will pass their time in play, dances and amusements. Thoughts of Last Judgment, Purgatory and Hell never entered their minds.

The Catholic missionary, who was trying to convert the Chumash to his own religion, disapproved that theirs did not include a hell. Until the Spanish arrived, however, the Chumash had good reason to believe that they could get along with the spirit world and that they had no reason to fear eternal torment. Their ancestors had lived in harmony with nature for thousands of years.

The Chumash way of life was based on respect for the earth and the plants and animals that they used for food. Unfortunately, that way of life proved to be very fragile when a new group of people arrived who had quite different plans for the Chumash's homeland. ▲

This is a painting of the Mission San Gabriel Arcangel, by Oriana Day. The Catholic missions ended the traditional Chumash way of life. Indians at the missions were forced to perform basic slave labor and convert to Catholicism.

CHAPTER 4

Spanish Rule

For about 200 years after the first Spanish ship sailed into the Santa Barbara Channel in 1542, the Chumash were more or less left alone. The Spanish conquered Mexico and Peru, where they enslaved the Indians and plundered their gold. The Chumash, however, had no gold, so the Spanish ignored them. Ships stopped for water and supplies, but no one moved onto their land or attempted to change their way of life.

Farther up the Pacific coast, in Alaska, the Russians were fishing and hunting sea otters. When the Russian hunters and trappers began moving south, the Spanish decided to make their presence felt in California. The

Spanish had arrived there first, after all, and they believed that the region and all its resources rightfully belonged to them. Their plan involved building Catholic missions to convert and control the Indians—along with military forts to make sure the missionaries' orders were followed.

The leader of the Spanish missionary effort was Father Junípero Serra. Born in Spain, Serra came to Mexico in 1749. He served in the Spanish missions in Baja California, then worked his way north. (Baja California is a peninsula in Mexico just south of the U.S. border. At the time, everything north of the Baja Peninsula was called Alta, or upper, California.) Serra founded his first mission in Alta California, which would eventually become part of the United States, in 1769. He called it Mission San Diego.

In August 1769, Captain Gaspar de Portolá led a voyage into Chumash territory by land from Mission San Diego. The group included 27 soldiers, 7 mule drivers, 2 priests, and 15 Christianized Indians. The Chumash welcomed them with baskets of seeds, fruit, fish, and meat, and the Spanish gave them beads, ribbon, and cloth in exchange. Confronted with the Indians' generosity, Lieutenant Pedro Fages wrote that "the gentleness and good disposition" of the Indians made him certain the Spanish would have no problem converting them to Christianity. Portolá continued north, and in 1770, he reached Monterey Bay. Serra arrived soon after and started a mission in Monterey before heading south to rejoin the Chumash.

The first mission that Serra built in Chumash territory was Mission San Luis Obispo de Tolosa, in 1772. Four more missions soon followed: San Buenaventura in 1782, Santa Bárbara in 1786, La Purísima Concepción in 1787, and Santa Ynéz in 1804.

Serra's goal was to convert the Chumash to Christianity and have the Indians do all the work on the missions. But few Chumash were interested in giving up their freedom and their beliefs to work for the priests. The Spanish soldiers were not concerned with what the Indians wanted, however; they simply rounded up the Chumash by force. Once they were imprisoned in the missions, the Indians were trained in woodworking, tilemaking, farming, weaving, and pottery making. They also began building aqueducts to carry water from the mountains for farming.

By 1789, 307 *neophytes*, as the Christianized Indians were called by the Spanish settlers, were working at Mission Santa Bárbara. One of their first tasks was to build new

homes for the priests, and eventually themselves. The mission buildings were made of adobe, a mixture of clay, straw, and water. The adobe bricks were shaped in wooden molds, and when dried in the sun they became rock-hard. The roofs were made of clay tiles or woven reeds. The adobe bricks were

This modern-day museum exhibit portrays daily life in a traditional Chumash village before the arrival of Spanish missionaries.

so tough and durable that many of these simple but elegant structures are still standing today.

The houses at the Santa Bárbara mission were surrounded by an eight-foot wall, and the Indians were locked in at night. Though the Chumash were imprisoned and treated as slaves, the Spanish settlers seemed to think that they were doing the Indians a favor by teaching them their way of life. One mission historian wrote, "The Indians, we can imagine, must have felt like lords in their neat and spacious homes which were so much more attractive and safe than the filthy huts they had inhabited as pagans."

The Chumash were actually much cleaner people than the newcomers. The Indians' daily sweat lodge ritual left them cleansed and purified. When they began living on the missions, however, many of them became very sick. The Spaniards brought with them a number of diseases that were much more dangerous to the Chumash than to themselves. Because the diseases were totally new to the region, the Indians' bodies had no resistance to them. Common colds turned into pneumonia or tuberculosis, and more serious illnesses such as measles, chicken pox, smallpox, and syphilis usually led to death. After 13 years, 40 percent of all the

continued on page 56

For the Spanish missionaries, converting the Chumash to Catholicism was not a simple matter. Even after the Indians were living at the missions and performing labor for the Spanish, they still maintained many beliefs that the Spanish disapproved of. The following story was told to ethnologist John P. Harrington by a Chumash Indian and later published in December's Child: A Book of Chumash Oral Narratives (1975), *edited by Thomas C. Blackburn. It reveals the wide gulf that still remained between the two cultures early in the 20th century.*

Two Men Fly at Santa Inez

At a place a short distance south of Santa Inez Mission there is a bank where they once dug lime for the building of the mission. The priest sent some Indians to dig lime there one time, and ordered others to carry it to the mission and still others to burn it. There were two island men digging lime there at the top of the bank, and the others told them not to talk too loudly or something might happen to them, but they paid no attention. Suddenly they heard a sound like an explosion and everyone looked up. They saw a cloud and in the cloud there was an animal that looked like a serpent. It had a big head with a tuft on it like a quail, but they could not see what the tuft was made of. The two islanders were carried off by the cloud. One finally fell near the mission while the other was carried as far as the Llano Grande.

Now two or three alcaldes (mission officials) had been there watching the workmen, and one of them, a man by the name of Manuel, was very much of a tattletale. He went and told the priest what had happened, and the priest summoned the two men (who were unhurt) and asked them what they had done. They answered that they had done nothing. The priest said, "I would have been very frightened if I had seen that." "We got scared and flew," the two workmen said. The priest said, "I'm a priest, but if I get scared I can't fly!" He admonished them not to do anything like that again, since that was an act of the devil and not of a human being, and they resumed their work.

continued from page 53

Indian converts were dead. Disease quickly spread through the villages of the free Indians as well. Often the survivors had no place to go but the missions, where they were exposed to an even greater threat of illness.

The military garrisons were another source of trouble. Many of the soldiers were deserters, mutineers, or criminals who had been sent to California from Mexico as a punishment. They routinely raped Chumash women and killed anyone who tried to interfere with their acts of violence and cruelty. Although the Chumash men were experienced warriors, they did not have guns and were no match for the Spaniards.

Indians who tried to run away from the missions were captured and put in prisons that they had been forced to build themselves. Other punishments included being put in structures called stocks. These humiliating devices were large wooden frames with holes to lock the head, feet, or hands. The persons being punished were locked in the stocks in the middle of the village where everyone could see them. Indians were also publicly whipped for their crimes.

These painful and humiliating punishments were especially upsetting to the Chumash. In their own society, the Indians had solved disputes without punishment. Individuals or villages often took revenge on each other through violence, but most local disputes were resolved by paying the victim a sum of money agreed on with the help of a wot. The prisons and harsh punishments introduced by the Spaniards were totally foreign to the Chumash.

Some of the priests were distressed by the way that the Indians were treated. The priests had hoped to help the Indians by teaching them their own religion and culture, which they considered superior to the Chumash's. But it was clear to even the most committed missionaries that the Indians were not better off as disease-ridden slaves. One Franciscan friar complained that "for the slightest things the [Indians] receive heavy floggings, are shackled, and put in the stocks, and treated with so much cruelty that they are kept whole days without a drink of water." For defending the Indians, the friar was arrested and declared insane.

When more Europeans moved to the area to start ranches, the missions lent them Chumash laborers. The missions kept the money they charged the settlers for the Indians' labor. Most white people became accustomed to having all their work done by Indians. One priest wrote that the whites "are so lazy and indolent that they know nothing more than to ride on horseback. Labor of any kind they regard as dishonorable. They are of the opinion that only Indians ought to work."

In 1801, the Chumash rebelled after a Chumash woman at Mission Santa Bárbara saw a spirit in a vision. The spirit told her that the Chumash should return to their old way of life. The rebellion was quickly crushed.

In 1824, however, the Chumash rose up in a much larger rebellion that spread to include the inmates of three missions. The uprising started at Mission Santa Ynéz. After one of the Indians was given a particularly brutal beating, the Santa Ynéz Chumash struck back. They set fire to the mission buildings and attacked the army post with bows and arrows. The revolt spread to La Purísima Concepción, where 200 Chumash seized control from the six Spanish soldiers on guard. The rebels' numbers quickly swelled to 400, as Indians from neighboring missions joined the war party.

A month later, 100 soldiers arrived from Mexico with a cannon. They executed seven Chumash men and imprisoned several others. At Mission Santa Bárbara, the Chumash had also revolted. When the Mexican soldiers arrived, the Chumash held them off

*Lucrecia Garcia,
a member of the
Barbareno Chumash,
was photographed
almost 90 years ago.
Like most of her fellow
Chumash, she had
abandoned traditional
Chumash attire for more
modern clothing.*

for a few hours with bows and arrows, then fled east to the hills.

Fifty armed soldiers were sent after the runaways to try to capture them and return them to *bondage*. The Spanish soldiers eventually caught up with the Chumash in the San Joaquin Valley, and a battle ensued at Buena Vista Lake. Some Chumash were killed, but the rest escaped to the San Emigdio hills, where they met with fellow fugitives from La Purísima and Santa Ynéz.

Finally the Chumash were caught between two groups of Spanish soldiers, 63 from Santa Bárbara and 50 from Monterey. A priest, Father Sárria, convinced the Indians to return to the missions rather than continue fighting. Some of the local Indians were taken back to the coast as well. But not all of the runaways were captured. Some continued to live free in the mountains.

Life in the mountains was difficult, however. As white ranchers took over the countryside, there was less and less for the Indians to eat. If they killed a single cow, the ranchers would *massacre* an entire village: men, women, children, and old people. Disease still continued to ravage the population of all California Indians. By the early 1800s, the Indian population in California had dropped from about 300,000—the number at the time the first Spanish settlers arrived—to less than 30,000.

The days of mission rule would soon end, but there would be little relief for the Chumash. After Mexico won independence from Spain, the Mexican government decided to take control of California away from the church and turn the mission lands over to civilians. In 1827, the Chumash were officially freed by Mexico. But their old society was gone. Most of the Chumash continued to live at the missions. With their former way of life now completely destroyed, mission life was the only existence that they knew. ▲

Modern-day Chumash have done much to restore and preserve their traditional way of life. Chumash historian, singer, and storyteller Vincent Tumamait (pictured here) is a leader in the movement to protect the Chumash heritage.

CHAPTER 5

"A War of Extermination"

In 1833, the Mexican government took possession of the vast landholdings that had previously been under mission control. A new law called the Provisional Regulation for the Emancipation of the Mission Indians awarded half the land of each mission to the Indians who had lived there. To protect the Chumash from greedy ranchers, the law stated that the Chumash's land could never be sold to anyone else.

Unfortunately, Mexican ranchers took over most of the land anyway. Few Chumash families could make a living on their

63

individual plots. Many simply abandoned their land, receiving nothing for it because it could not be sold. A few of the Chumash continued to live at the missions. Some went to small towns to look for work, while others moved farther inland to live among unconverted Indians. But most of the Chumash simply stayed where they were and worked for the ranchers.

Though life under mission rule had been a disaster for the Chumash, the priests had at least shown some concern for the Indians' well-being. The missionaries had taught the Indians useful skills, and they truly believed that they were helping the Chumash by sharing their religion with them. But the wealthy ranchers, who now owned vast tracts of land on which huge herds of cattle and other animals roamed, cared nothing about the souls of the Chumash people. The ranchers considered the Indians to be nothing more than a cheap source of labor.

At the missions, the Chumash had learned many trades because they made everything used there and grew their own food. But the new ranches produced nothing but beef. Everything else the owners needed was imported. Because all the Chumash did at the ranches was tend animals, they soon lost their other skills.

The priests had also allowed the Chumash to go home occasionally to visit their former villages. As ranch employees, however, they were never allowed to leave. For many of the Indians, this meant that the last ties to their old way of life were finally broken.

In 1836, a visitor to the mission at Santa Bárbara noted, "The Mission is a large and deserted looking place, the outbuildings are going to ruin and everything gives the impression of decayed grandeur." The commander of the soldiers posted at Santa Bárbara, Captain José de la Guerra y Noriega, became a wealthy man. He personally owned more than 50,000 cattle and 300,000 acres of land. By contrast, only 246 Chumash remained in the Santa Bárbara area in 1839. The Chumash's homeland was now occupied primarily by cattle.

The big ranches flourished through the 1830s and 1840s. During this time, there was still a place for the Chumash in the California economy. But in 1848, two important events heralded the beginning of the end. In January, gold was discovered in California. The next month, Mexico surrendered control of California to the United States as a result of Mexico's crushing defeat by U.S. troops in the Mexican War. Thousands of white Americans immediately poured into California in

search of gold, and most of them settled there permanently. By 1850, California had become an official U.S. state, the 31st in the Union.

While the Mexicans had used the Indians as workers, the new settlers simply wanted them out of the way. In a message to the

An early 20th-century photograph shows a Chumash couple in front of the Catholic mission at Santa Barbara.

California legislature in 1851, Governor Burnett bluntly stated "that a war of extermination would continue to be waged until the Indian race should become extinct."

The new settlers did everything in their power to make Burnett's gruesome prediction come true. White Californians massacred whole villages. By 1910, the population of California Indians had dropped by 90 percent from what it had been in 1770. The Indians who did not starve or die of disease either tried to survive in the mountains or became servants or wage laborers for the whites. Many lived in conditions verging on slavery. The California legislature passed a law that allowed any white person to have an Indian imprisoned for *vagrancy*—without proof. The Indian was then auctioned as an unpaid laborer for weeks or months at a time. Another law allowed whites to buy Indian children from their parents for years at a time, during which the children were forced to work without pay.

Abuses against Indians by whites almost always went unpunished. The California Indians had virtually no legal protection. The Chumash and other Native Americans in the region were not allowed to defend themselves in court. They were wards of the U.S. government, which was supposed to represent them in legal matters. When word of atrocities against the Indians finally reached Washington, D.C., however, it was usually too late for anything to be done.

After whites took away most Indian lands in California, the U.S. government did grant small pieces of land called *reservations* to some of the tribes. The government also sent special *agents* to protect the Indians' interests. Often the people sent from Washington to help the Indians were corrupt. With little accountability, the agents easily stole money meant for the Indians and committed other abuses.

An 1856 article in a San Francisco newspaper described one example of such abuse against a group that lived north of the Chumash. It is unclear from the article which tribe was involved because most California Indians were referred to by whites simply as Diggers.

Some of the agents, and nearly all of the employees, we are informed, of one of these reservations at least, are daily and nightly engaged in kidnapping the younger portion of the females, for the vilest of purposes. The wives and daughters of the defenceless Diggers are prostituted before the very eyes of their husbands and fathers, by these civilized monsters, and they dare not resent the insult, or even complain of the hideous outrage.

The following article gives an example of the failure of the white legal system to provide any protection for the Chumash. Entitled "Murder in Santa Barbara," this story appeared in a Sacramento newspaper in 1851:

> An Indian was murdered in Santa Barbara, recently, under circumstances which call loudly for the establishment of a Vigilance Committee in that place. He was called from his house by a Sonorian, whose name we did not learn, and who without any provocation whatever, plunged a knife into his heart, killing him instantly. Some four or five Indians were present, witnesses to the transaction, and they pursued the murderer, caught him and carried him before a magistrate. Will it be believed that he was almost immediately released from custody, because our laws will not allow an Indian to testify against a white man? The Indians in this part of the State, in the main a harmless race, are left entirely at the mercy of every ruffian in the country, and if something is not done for their protection, the race will shortly become extinct.

The Chumash were not granted a reservation of their own until 1901. They were given only 75 acres of land near the Santa Ynéz mission, the last mission to house Chumash families in the region. The tiny plot of land could support only about 50 permanent residents at the time, though the number would grow to around 100 in the second half of the 20th century.

continued on page 72

The flood of white American settlers who moved to California follow-ing the gold rush in the 1850s made life extremely difficult for the Chumash. After their traditional hunting territory was taken away, the Indians were often forced to kill the ranchers' cattle to survive. The whites responded to such "depredations" by massacring whole villages. The following newspaper article, originally published in San Francisco in 1860, provides just one example of many docu-mented massacres. It was reprinted in 1974 in The Destruction of California Indians, *edited by Robert F. Heizer.*

Horrible Massacre of 200 Indians in Humboldt County

By the steamer *Columbia*, which arrived this forenoon from the North, we have tidings of a terrible butchery, by a band of white murderers, of the Indians around Humboldt Bay. Mr. Lord, the express messenger of Wells, Fargo & Co., favors us with the following statement of the massacre:

Between three and four o'clock on Sunday morning last, (26 February,) an attack was made by a party of white men, upon Indians at several villages around Humboldt Bay. At Indian Island, opposite the town of Eureka, and distant but a few hundred yards, more than 40 Indians were killed, three-fourths of the number being women and children. On the beach, south of the entrance to the bay, forty or fifty Indians were also killed. Report says all that were there—every one—was killed. It is also reported, and is no doubt true, that a simultaneous attack was made upon the villages on Eel river. From what was known in Eureka not less than two hundred Indians—men, women and children—were killed on this Sabbath morning.

It is believed that the farmers and graziers of Eel river county, who have suffered from Indian depredations, during the past year, were the men who performed the deed. The cause assigned is, that the coast Indians furnished arms and ammunition to those in the mountains, and gave them asylum, when hard pressed by the volunteers. They have been seen to take large quantities of beef from the mountains to their houses nearer the settlements. Most of the people at Eureka and vicinity were bitter in their denunciation of this wholesale butchery.

J. A. Lord

Another writer reported:

This is but the commencement of an Indian war in that section of the country. An intelligent Indian told the people of Eureka, that the white men had killed his wives and children, and he had nothing more to live for; and he was going to the mountains with what few of his tribe were left, to fight against the whites.

J. R. D.

continued from page 69

Peter Zavala, dressed in traditional Chumash attire, and his daughter Takaita were photographed in 1989 at a special program to celebrate Chumash customs.

Several Chumash families live on this reservation today. Many of the women work as domestic servants or grow vegetables to sell. The men often seek jobs around the town of Santa Ynez. In the early 1900s, the U.S. government ran a school on the reservation. The school closed after a short time, however, and Chumash children began attending public school in Santa Ynez. These children became the first Chumash people to learn English. After the last people who spoke the Chumash language died in the 1920s, the first language of most Chumash was Spanish. In the 1930s and 1940s, some of these children began attending high school, but many had to drop out because their families depended on them to work.

In recent years the Santa Ynez Chumash have made great advances academically and economically. A Chumash business council runs a profitable bingo parlor and a housing program funded by the U.S. government. Chumash groups—such as the United Chumash Council, the Brotherhood of the Tomol, the Southern Owl Clan, and the Ventura United Chumash—have become powerful voices for Chumash interests. The groups have won legal battles to preserve sacred and historic Chumash sites. They have also invited scholars to teach classes at the reservation on archaeology and Chumash history. Armed with their new skills, the Chumash today play an important role in current research about their own past. They work as computer analysts and field and laboratory assistants with archaeologists and other scholars.

Archaeologists first became interested in the Chumash in the 1870s. Tons of artifacts were removed by early expeditions. One group from France made off with 3,000 artifacts for the Musée de l'Homme (Museum of Man) in Paris. The scientific excursions were soon followed by looters, who plundered thousands of objects to be sold to curious Europeans. One man boasted of assisting in the removal of 30 tons of relics from the Santa Barbara area alone, to be sold as curios.

Laws passed in the 1970s now protect Chumash religious sites, cemeteries, important plant areas, and the locations of ancient villages. Now the interests and views of the Chumash people must be taken into account before any digging or construction can take place in these areas. The Chumash also have a representative on the California Native Heritage Commission. This representative must be consulted whenever a Chumash burial site is uncovered.

Barely two centuries after whites began settling in the Chumash's traditional homeland, pollution and other environmental problems have grown to crisis proportions. As Californians confront the serious problems they have created in such a short time, respect continues to grow for California's previous inhabitants, who were able to live in harmony with their environment for thousands of years. It is only fitting that today Chumash people are emerging as some of the leading spokespeople on environmental issues in the region. There is a great deal that all Americans can learn from a people whose civilization thrived for so many centuries before the arrival of the first white settlers. ▲

GLOSSARY

agent   the official representative of the U.S. government to an Indian tribe

anthropologist   a person who studies people and their cultures

archaeologist   a scientist who studies the remains of past civilizations

barter   trade

bondage   slavery

century   a period of 100 years

coiffure   hairstyle

excavate   uncover by digging

grove   a piece of land covered with trees

ingenious   clever

massacre   to murder a large group of defenseless people

mission   a religious center founded by Christians trying to convert the native population to their faith

neopyhte   a new member of a religious group

ocher   an earthy substance that contains iron ore and has a rich red or yellow color

reservation   a piece of land defined by the U.S. government as the legal territory of an Indian tribe

shaman   a religious leader with magic powers

tantalizing   stimulating interest or desire

vagrancy   having no home; wandering the streets without a job

CHRONOLOGY

27,000 to 12,000 years ago   First human beings come to North America

10,000 years ago   Ancestors of the Chumash known as the Millingstone people develop civilization on California coast

3,000 years ago   Chumash civilization emerges

October 10, 1542   First contact with Europeans occurs with visit of Spanish expedition led by Juan Cabrillo

1772   Junípero Serra founds first mission in Chumash territory, Mission San Luis Obispo de Tolosa

1782   Mission San Buenaventura founded

1786   Mission Santa Bárbara founded

1787   Mission La Purísima Concepción founded

1801   Rebellion occurs at Mission Santa Bárbara

1804   Mission Santa Ynéz founded

1824   Several hundred Indians rebel in violent uprising at three missions; soldiers sent from Mexico chase Chumash into the hills

1827   Mexican government gives Chumash their freedom; most remain on missions

1833   Mexican government takes control of mission lands; half is given to Indians, but most is taken away by ranchers, who employ Chumash to tend cattle

1848   Gold is discovered in California, prospectors flood in; U.S. takes control of California after victory in Mexican War

1850   California becomes 31st U.S. state

1901   Chumash granted tiny reservation near Santa Ynéz mission

INDEX

ABOUT THE AUTHOR

MARTIN SCHWABACHER is the author of *Magic Johnson, Basketball Wizard*, in Chelsea House's JUNIOR WORLD BIOGRAPHIES series. He grew up in Minneapolis, Minnesota, and currently works as an editor and freelance writer in New York City.

PICTURE CREDITS